TRACTORS

David and Penny Glover

WAYLAND

First published in 2007 by Wayland

Copyright © Wayland 2007

This paperback edition published in 2011 by Wayland

Wayland
338 Euston Road
London NW1 3BH

Wayland
Level 17/207 Kent Street
Sydney, NSW 2000

Editor: Camilla Lloyd
Editorial Assistant: Katie Powell
Designer: Elaine Wilkinson
Picture Researcher: Diana Morris

Picture Acknowledgements: The author and publisher would like to thank the following for allowing these pictures to be reproduced in this publication: John Deere: Cover, 1, 4, 5, 7, 9, 11, 12, 13, 16b, 17, 18; Humphrey Evans/Sylvia Cordaiy PL/Alamy: 14, Glyn Thomas/Alamy: 15t, All Over Photography/Alamy: 15b, Greenshoots Communications/Alamy: 16t, Bartomeu Amengual/Alamy: 19, Dennis Macdonald/Alamy: 20, 21; Nick Wheeler/Corbis: 22, Paul Souders/Corbis 10b; Holt Studios/FLPA Images: 8, 10t; Chris Saltberger/Image Bank/Getty Images: 6.

With special thanks to John Deere.

British Library Cataloguing in Publication Data
Glover, David, 1953 Sept. 4-
       Tractors. - (On the go)
       1. Tractors - Juvenile literature
       I. Title II. Glover, Penny
       629.2'252

ISBN 978 0 7502 6710 6

Printed in China

Wayland is a division of Hachette Children's Books

Contents

What are tractors?   4

Tractor parts   6

In the cab   8

Tractor wheels   10

What makes it go?   12

Tractors at work   14

Special jobs   16

Tractor safety   18

Tractor fun   20

Old tractors   22

Tractor words   23

Quiz answers   24

Index   24

What are tractors?

Tractors are vehicles that move things. Most tractors work on farms. They pull **ploughs** and other farm machines. A farmer can hook a **trailer** to the tractor to pull a heavy **load**.

tractor

trailer

Some tractors can lift and push, as well as pull. This tractor is lifting straw.

lifting arm

Tractor quiz

Where do most tractors work?

5

Tractor parts

The tractor driver sits in the **cab**. This is high up so he can see all around. The tractor's **engine** is at the front, under the **hood**.

cab

hood

hitch

wheels

The tractor's **hitch** is at the back. This is where the tractor hooks onto the things it pulls.

This tractor has a **scoop** to lift sand and soil.

scoop

spotlights

When it gets dark, the driver can turn on **spotlights** so he or she can see to work.

Tractor quiz

What is under the tractor's hood?

In the cab

control switches

steering wheel

The driver turns the front wheels to the right or left with the steering wheel. This makes the tractor turn.

Levers, switches and buttons work the tractor parts.

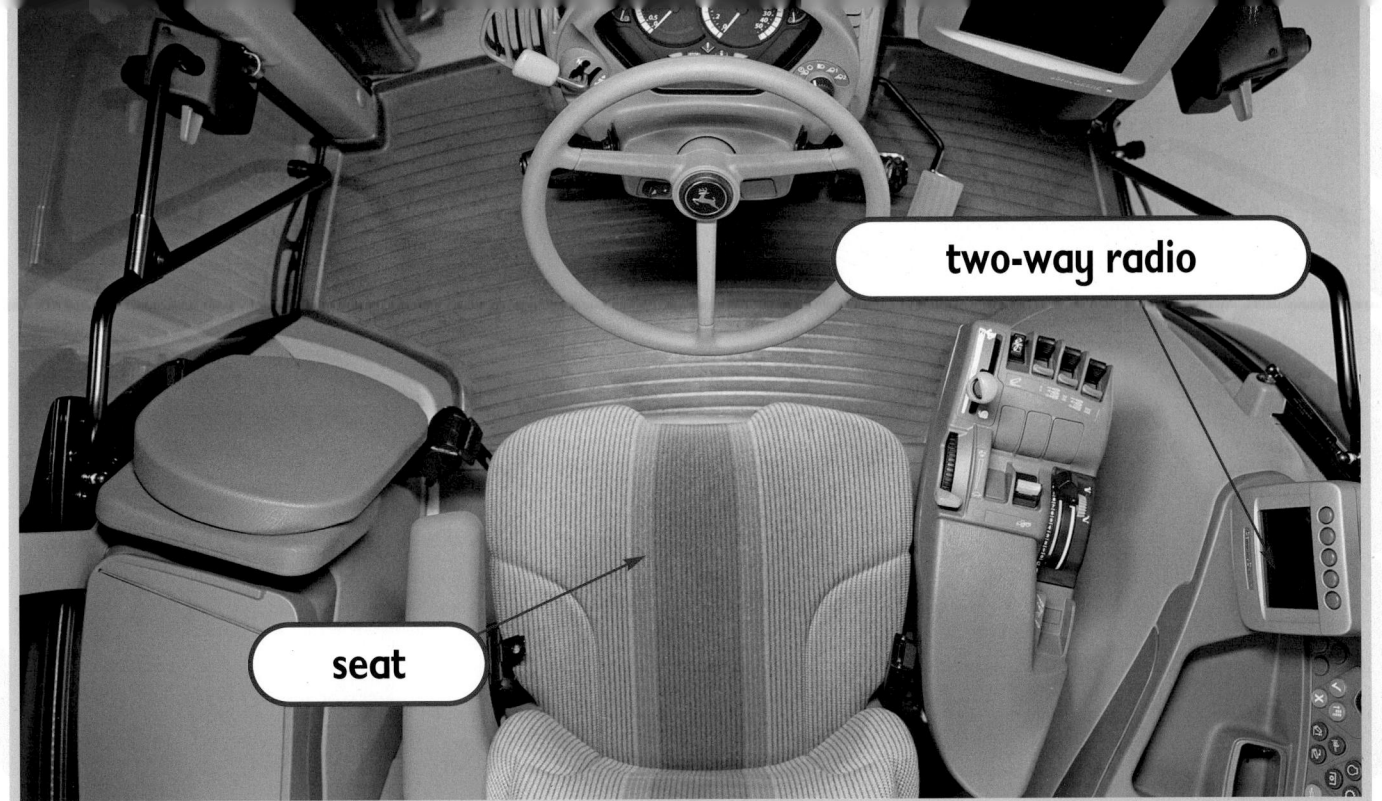

two-way radio

seat

The driver's seat is comfortable. The driver sometimes sits in the tractor all day to plough a field. The driver can talk to other people with a **two-way radio**.

Tractor quiz

How can a tractor driver talk to other people while he works?

Tractor wheels

The tractor has big wheels so it can cross soft mud and rough ground. Small wheels would sink or get stuck. A rod called an **axle** fixes each wheel to the tractor.

axle

tread

Tractor wheels have thick rubber tyres to grip the ground. The tyres have deep **tread** so they don't slip. This works like the grips on the bottom of a pair of trainers.

Tractor quiz

What are tractor tyres made from?

What makes it go?

engine

The tractor's engine makes it go. It turns the wheels to move the tractor along.

The engine runs on **diesel fuel**. The driver fills the fuel tank from a tank in the farmyard.

The tractor's engine also powers the different machines the tractor pulls. This tractor is pulling a grass cutter.

grass cutter

Tractor quiz
What fuel does a tractor engine run on?

Tractors at work

blade

plough

When there is a field to plough, the farmer hitches the plough to the tractor. The tractor pulls the plough across the field.

The plough breaks up the soil. Then the farmer can plant the seeds.

Tractor quiz
What does a plough do?

fertiliser spreader

If there is a
trailer to pull,
or fertiliser
to spread,
a tractor can
do that too.

Tractor to the rescue! When another
vehicle gets stuck in the mud or
breaks down, a tractor can pull it.

Special jobs

lifeboat

Some tractors do jobs away from the farm. This tractor pulls a lifeboat and its crew in and out of the water.

This tractor lifts logs in the forest.

This mini-tractor is cutting the grass in a garden.

Tractor quiz
What might a tractor lift in the forest?

Tractor safety

Old-fashioned tractors did not have a cab. If the tractor rolled over the driver could be trapped underneath.

safety cab

Tractors are slower than cars. When a tractor drives along a road, a flashing light warns car drivers it is there.

flashing light

Tractor quiz
Why were old tractors dangerous?

Tractor fun

Sometimes tractors take part in pulling contests. It's a tractor tug of war! Special tractors with powerful engines compete to pull the heaviest load.

Children can ride tractors too. This tractor is pedal-powered. It does not have an engine.

Tractor quiz

What do the tractors do in a pulling contest?

Old tractors

Before tractors were invented horses pulled ploughs.

The first tractors were powered by steam. They were called **traction engines**. Then the diesel engine was invented.

Tractor words

axle
The rod through the centre of a wheel.

cab
The part of the tractor where the driver sits.

diesel
The fuel a tractor engine uses to make it go.

engine
The part of the tractor that makes it move.

fuel
Something that burns inside an engine to make it work.

hitch
The part that hooks the tractor to a trailer, a plough or other farm machines.

hood
The engine cover.

load
Something you lift or carry.

plough
The farm machine a tractor pulls to break up the soil.

scoop
The big bucket for scooping up sand or soil.

spotlights
The lights on the cab of the tractor that let the driver see when it is dark.

traction engine
The name of the first steam powered tractors.

trailer
The part that is hooked on to the tractor to carry the load.

tread
Deep grooves on the tractor's tyres that grip soft ground.

two-way radio
The radio in a tractor which lets the driver talk to other people.

Quiz answers

Page 5 On farms.

Page 7 The engine.

Page 9 With a two-way radio.

Page 11 Rubber.

Page 13 Diesel fuel.

Page 14 It breaks up the soil.

Page 17 Logs.

Page 19 Because they did not have a cab to keep the driver safe.

Page 21 They compete to pull the heaviest load.

Index

A
axle 10

C
cab 6, 18
control switches 8

D
diesel fuel 12

E
engine 6, 12, 22

F
farm 4, 12
fertiliser 15
fertiliser spreader 15
flashing light 19

G
grass cutter 13

H
hitch 6
hood 6, 7

L
lifeboat 16
load 4

M
mini-tractor 17

P
pedal-powered tractor 21
plough 4, 9, 14

S
scoop 7
spotlights 7
steering wheel 8

T
traction engine 22
tractor contests 20
trailer 4
tread 11
two-way radio 9
tyres 11

W
wheels 6, 8, 10, 11, 12